30 Days of Inspiration

A Guide to Personal Fulfilment in Just One Month

By Terrie Anderson

An Awakening to Your Inner Self

Realise Your Personal Potential

Be in Control of Your Own Destiny

30 Days of Inspiration

Published By

Easy Online Portals Pty Ltd
GPO Box 865
Brisbane 4001 Australia

Enquiries to Information@easyonlineportals.com

Cover Design by Rudy Pauwels

ISBN 978-0-9807248-0-6

Dedication

This book is dedicated to the amazing Masters that I have worked with, thank you for so many years of success and happiness.

In particular I would like to acknowledge substantial contributions from the works and inspiration of:

Stuart Wilde

Louise Hay

Dr Wayne Dyer

John Kehoe

Thank you to Michael Brown (Secret of the Andes) whose book started my quest, and to James Redfield (The Celestine Prophecy) whose principles I use daily with fabulous results.

I would also like to thank Rudy Pauwels and EasyDog for their ongoing love, inspiration and support in my mission to reach out to people around the world, and inspire those I meet to show how amazing they really are!

Foreword

Welcome to our time together to guide you through some steps that will ensure you are ready for the success and happiness you deserve.

Let me first define what *SUCCESS* and *HAPPINESS* mean for the purpose of this guide.

Success is not just about money, although for many of us to be successful, wealth is part of our goals. There are many people whose goals do not include money, they can meet their basic needs and their goals are spiritual, physical or mental. Success is the consistent achievement of goals that you set for yourself, nothing more. If you regularly achieve what you plan for yourself, then you are very successful.

Happiness is having peace of mind, in feeling positive about life in general, and in being enough in control of your life and your reactions to have a life filled with easy smiles and a sense of purpose and joy of fulfilment. Achieving what you want in life is a huge contributor to happiness. If we are always failing to meet our own goals then we will feel unhappy. A happy person can overcome any obstacles and recover from adversities much easier and faster than others. So, success and happiness go hand in hand.

This guide will also begin to open your mind to easily understand the Laws of Attraction and Abundance.

Each day for the next 30 days I encourage you to read just the appropriate page for that day, if you miss a day then just pick up where you left off. After you read the page, please try and take the actions as soon as possible. In fact, I recommend that you do not proceed, until you have taken action, or have a written plan of when you will. The guide will not deliver the results you want unless you also take action.

There are some organisational tasks that will take longer than a day, for these I would suggest that you make a plan on the day and put these plans in your agenda to complete the tasks. It is important not to miss out a step, unless you are already doing that particular step well. If you miss steps, your results will only be mediocre, you will get small improvements every day, but if you complete the full guide then you will have a real shift to a success based lifestyle in just one month!

At the end of each day I have provided you a special page for your personal notes, I encourage you to use this for future reference. It can also be a record of your achievements day by day. You could record there what you did that day to achieve the step. This is very motivational, as you can look back anytime, and see how much you have already achieved!

I hope you enjoy our next 30 Days together, and know that if you complete the guide you will have many additional free hours every week. You can then use these hours to relax, pamper yourself, or take steps towards your goals. The results from our trials of this 30 Day guide with approximately 100 people have been absolutely fantastic!

Now, let us start, and get you on the path to a lifestyle, and a mindset, geared for success and a happier life!

Terrie

Visit Terrie at *www.terrieanderson.com*

The Beginning..........

The journey to a success mentality can take just one month!

Tomorrow is the first day of the rest of your life. Cliché maybe, but ever so true!

Few people are successful and happy, but those few that are, will plan their days to maximise their enjoyment and productivity, and to minimise negative impacts.

Now I don't mean for a second that you should be boring, and not have impulsive moments. That would not be my kind of day at all. However, if you have a plan, then the opportunity to have positive impulsive experiences is increased.

How can this be?

Well, if we know where we want to go, and what we want to achieve today – then when an impulsive opportunity arises we immediately know if it takes us away from our goals, makes no difference or even helps us get closer! Then we know what to do in most situations that arise, with a relaxed state of mind, confidence and a smile.

So, what do you want to achieve tomorrow?

To achieve this, what frame of mind need you be in?

How should you be dressed to improve your chances of success?

What time do you need to awaken to ensure you look and feel good, and are where you need to be on time?

An example:

Let's say you want the guy, or girl, at the bus stop to notice you, and you want to apply for a new position in another department.

You will need to be in a positive frame of mind, so you need good sleep, be calm and radiate positive energy. You definitely need to be smiling.

Your dress needs to be interesting, yet professional, to achieve both objectives. You should be comfortable but feel amazing, make sure that outfit is ready to go the evening before! You know shoes cleaned, clothing ironed and brushed etc.

Lastly, plan your schedule to arrive at the bus stop 5-6 minutes early, in a calm state of mind and say 'Hi 'to that guy or girl, ask them what they hope their day will bring.

My Notes

Did you make a plan? If you didn't, it is going to get trickier as we go along, so maybe you better go back and have a bash at Day One again!

If you did, Congratulations! You have taken the first step on a great journey that will amaze you with its rewards.

Have a look in the mirror today. What do you see? Does the person looking back at you match the image of a person who can achieve those goals? If they do, then that is sensational.

If not, then here is what we do.

Take a long look in the mirror and define where the mismatches are, between what you see, and what you believe the image should be.

Now one thing I can promise you - it is very unlikely to be anything physical. You are not too small, big, tall, short, ugly, pretty, or anything else. It is not affected by a big nose, crooked teeth, a birthmark, uneven ears, colour of skin, or any other thing that is part of your natural body. One qualifier here – if there is something wrong that is a sign of your neglect of yourself, then that can impact your image. For example, bad breath, or body odour due to unclean hygiene.

Unless you believe you already have the right image that fits your goal, then I want you to look at the things you could change and start on a plan to change them. If your hair is a disaster, make an appointment with a hairdresser (or if finance is tight, a plan to save enough money to do it). If your clothes are too tight, or too big or inappropriate - the same applies – change it, or save to change it. If your shoes are shabby or dirty, repair or clean them.

Image is important; it reflects our self esteem and confidence. It gives other people a first impression. Mostly though, it helps us feel more confident, more powerful, when we know we look like a person who should achieve the sort of goals we want.

Remember a builder should look like a builder and not a Grand Prince at court, but he doesn't have to look like a shabby builder – he needs to look like a professional one to be successful!

If you have money issues, do not despair. There are some excellent recycled, good label clothing shops in most cities. Here you can buy fabulous clothes for a tiny fraction of their original price, and look like a star if you want to!

Image is how we show who we are!

PS. Don't forget your plan for tomorrow; you don't want to waste a day!

My Notes

Don't worry too much if you haven't got it right yet, I have every confidence that you will, because now you have a plan.

Now, I want to ask you to plan a bit more. I want you to think about this year ahead. What do you want to achieve? Not just material objects, but also emotionally, spiritually, in your relationships, anywhere in your life really.

I would like you to take a piece of paper and write down just the 10 most important things you would like to achieve by the same date next year. You can be a bit brave and adventurous here, be a bit bold and stretch yourself. Do not put down things over which you have no influence or control. I.e. you may not list something on behalf of someone else. This is all about you, so it is ok to be completely selfish, and proud of it.

Once you have written this list, read it through carefully three times, then fold it and put it in a safe place where you can find it again on the same day next year. Put a note in your agenda to view it again next year.

You will have to trust me, but if you do this sensibly and in a committed frame of mind, then you will be very surprised and happy next year when you reopen your piece of paper and read it.

The average person will achieve at least 50% of their goals, even if they don't review that piece of paper. Many people I have worked with have achieved 70-80% year on year! A few, and I am one of them, can honestly say they have achieved 100% of their goals every year for many, many years.

My goals were quite bold things like I want to double my income, which actually at the time of writing seemed impossible, but I did it every year for the four years that it was my goal! My list always has a mix of quality of life, money, adventure and relationship goals. This seems to give me a nice balance across my life – no point for me in being very rich, or very powerful, if I am lonely.

People with balanced goals and lives are much happier than those with just a money focus, not that there is anything wrong with money. I have found it is not dirty, does not bring sadness, and actually it is very useful to help yourself, and others, along the way, not to mention a nice lifestyle that can provide jobs for many people. Most importantly, having money allows you more choices.

So now, go make that list, and don't forget tomorrows plan too!

My Notes

Day 4   *It is Here Someplace!*

Is this you?

Are you somewhat disorganised? Or losing things regularly?

Do you forget to pay your bills, even though there is money in your bank?

Are you often apologising for forgetting things?

If not, then this will be a nice affirmation of what you are doing right.

If it is you, then let's get this sorted out. By now, you probably think I am getting a bit boring with all these plans and now organising things. But I want to share a secret – if you are reasonably well organised, you have more time to have fun!

I used to spend sometimes hours helping my partner find things he had lost, or solving an unpaid invoice because, well no one ever saw it. That is no more!

I am not a highly organised person, so I am going to tell you how to help this problem for people who hate organising stuff ☺

Let's start with paper and mail. Drawers, containers or even boxes, are fabulous organisers. They become sort of loose systems for everything.

When your mail comes in, have a drawer, or container where it ALWAYS goes immediately open or not. Just throw it there for now.

Have another place with 12 dividers, marked by month.

Have yet a few more spaces allocated for things like Information, Guarantees, Contracts, Tax. You need to keep these handy, like in a cupboard nearby. I have an inexpensive IKEA set of plywood filing drawers that hold 90% of my stuff with a tray on top for the incoming mail.

Now every week on a set day, e.g. every Monday evening, go to the inbox and see what is there. If it's a contract, stick it straight in the contract file, if it's a bill mark clearly date for payment and put it in a bills to pay folder IN that inbox. If it's a receipt, or paid bill, stick it in that month etc. This will take you about 10 minutes each week, and *surprise,* that takes care of your papers and bill paying.

Every week when you check your inbox, check bills to pay and take those with you tomorrow that need to be paid this week!

When you need something you will know approximately where it is, without searching for hours. It is not a perfect system, but if you hate filing (like I do) this minimises boring work, and makes it easy to do and follow. When you need something it is only a few minutes to locate it. Successful people are organised and minimise wasted time.

 Don't forget tomorrows plan, first day of the rest of your life remember!

My Notes

Yesterday, we looked at paper and mail.

You can use a similar system to clear your email, even if you get hundreds every day. The secret is not to let that Inbox grow too large, or all is lost.

If it is too large, and overwhelming to even contemplate starting, then I suggest hitting the delete button (after a quick check for anyone critical on the list like your boss, or the word URGENT). Then let everyone assume you had a hard drive failure, and you will be shocked that only about 10% of that original email ever comes back to you again ☺

Set up a simple set of files that are easy to store to....I suggest one for every month, plus a few identified for the common things you get every day and may need to recall.

I have each month, and then I have about 10 other folders for emails that I regularly need to recall, like e-invoices for the quarterly accounts, subscription data, legal issues and technical issues. Everything on which you are CC'd can be filtered to a separate Inbox, you probably don't need to read most of it.

Every day, when I open my email, I first delete things I don't need to open. There goes 50%, then I view and file every email appropriately, anything I cannot handle 'on the fly' I mark it and leave in my Inbox. I.e. Handle it and file it, or else leave it where I cannot forget it, this means only about 5% of my email needs to remain in my inbox!

Only check email at certain points of the day, do other stuff in between, and check at regular intervals. This makes for a better time management and focus. You will save time doing this.

Now you will be able to find your emails, especially if your email client has a good search function. Email mountains can eat our energy, and demotivate our day, we must ensure our email is a positive contributor and not a time eater.

Well, that's found simple solutions for two big black holes into which hours of our precious time can vanish!

Tomorrow we are going to look at similar systems for other stuff in your life – and you have to start thinking what you are going to do with all the free time you have gained back. The time you used to spend, every single day, agonising over trying to locate something you know you put someplace.

Do you have a diary, calendar or agenda? If not, why not? Because by Day 7 we are going to take a look on how that can add even more time to the free fun-time bank!

....and you do not need reminding about tomorrows plan.

My Notes

So we have looked at, and I hope you have worked on, papers and email.

Do you know something very interesting? Many friends, couples and families actually argue (even fight) over lost things, especially papers. Blame flies around like an angry bird, and causes very negative feelings and emotions.

Your home should be a safe haven of peace, and a fun place to be – so let's get finally organised.

That same system for the papers can also be adapted for 'things' too.

Designate cupboards, shelves, boxes, even rooms for specific purposes

I have a friend who loves to ski, he unfortunately broke his leg. Not on the black slopes like you would imagine – nope, he fell over the skis he left on his lounge room floor! End of the ski season for him, and it didn't even make a good story!

Out of the way places should be used to store things you rarely use, like the skis in summer. But put ALL the things related to skiing, or perhaps sport, in one place!

Do the same with all your stuff; put everything related to one area together. Your tools should be in one place, paint and brushes in another space (or box), your sporting gear grouped together, your car stuff on one shelf.

Same in the kitchen, and in your wardrobe. It is much faster to find the particular shirt you want in an organised wardrobe, and you know the amazing thing – once the initial sort is done – it takes no longer to hang the blue shirt with other blue shirts, or the long sleeved shirt with others (depending how you like to be organised) than to stuff it in at random. The 'find' speed however is almost instantaneous, compared to several minutes. In a day you can save an hour of time, and miles of frustration, by just knowing where everything is located. That is a lot of time you can now spend doing something amazing, or relaxing, instead!

It is a hassle to get it all done, but if you tackle one room, or type of stuff, at a time, let's say every Tuesday night, then in a few weeks, you will have hours more time every week to enjoy yourself! You will feel lighter, freer, and happier. It will be easier to be successful, as you will have better focus and more positive energy.

My Notes

How much stuff do you have around you that no longer, or rarely, serves a purpose?

A successful, happy person will keep only what they need around them, the rest is clutter that after awhile begins to own you.

Look in your wardrobe:

Are there clothes lurking in there you have not worn for a year? Why?

Are there things that do not fit, or are damaged?

Are there guilt starters, you know you bought it on sale, but after you knew you hated it?

Are there bad memory numbers, like the tie, or dress, you wore when your ex broke it off?

You need to get rid of anything that you do not use, no matter what it cost, or who gave it to you. If it is no longer useful – boof! Out it goes.

That applies to more than clothes; it applies to *everything* you own.

If you need to keep, for example kids things, for later when they grow up, store it in a labelled box someplace out of the way. Same goes for other memories you do not look at, use or review very often.

Clean out every cupboard, drawer, shed, attic and cellar. You can give it away to people who can use it, OR you can make some extra cash on sites like Easysell and eBay.

It is very simple - You cannot fly high, if you carry around everything you ever owned but no longer use! Get rid of them and be as free as possible.

If you only use those skis one week every year, then either make them an art form on the wall for the other 51 weeks, or sell them. Then rent new gear each year you ski, it is cheaper and more useful than storing old fashioned skis, and they date quickly!

You can apply this acid test to everything you own. Do I use it? If not, Why Not? Do I look at it regularly? Do I really need it? You will find a lot of things that you realise you don't need, or even want anymore.

After this clean out, you will feel lighter and more bouncy. You will have the pleasure of giving it to someone or getting in some unexpected cash. It is all positive!

My Notes

Hope your plan for today is an exciting one, and I just know you are going to achieve it!

Why should you run a good agenda or diary? And what makes an agenda good?

You should run an agenda so that your mind can relax, and it can focus on what is really important to you, instead of focussing on recalling minor details like which bill to pay, or call to make.

A good agenda is a holistic one, one that encompasses your whole life, and can be planned a year ahead. I use my Google calendar because I am online every day, and it will send me emails to remind me to do things. It is like an unpaid secretary.

A good agenda will include, the bills you need to pay (the regular ones can have repeating entries every month automatically), birthdays of your friends and family, special events, trips, notes about the day that are important to you, other peoples holidays that affect you. It should have all your meetings, important calls and to do's, and I put also my day plan in it. It is in short, your reliable assistant. I no longer bother to remember everything in my head; I deploy my mind onto other more interesting things.

Every day when I start work, my diary sends me an email with today's list of To-dos, my goals, any birthdays, events or holidays. Then it reminds me in a timely fashion of events throughout the day. It also stores my evening appointments, so I never have to apologise for forgetting a friend's dinner party, or child's special event.

Your friends will be impressed when you recall their special day, or remember that their son plays his first match today – and it is all the work of your faithful assistant who does it for you.

A diary will give you free thinking time, it will give you more peace and freedom, and above all it will ensure you can be on top of everything in your life without too much effort.

You however are an integral point in making this work, a few minutes of discipline to enter each event, means a huge weight off your shoulders and more time to smile and enjoy life knowing you won't mess up anything too badly by forgetting!

Trust me no one knows your agenda was the one to remember to order the roses for an anniversary, but you are the winner!

Make a plan to start using your agenda fully and holistically tomorrow!

My Notes

_____

_____

_____

_____

_____

_____

_____

_____

_____

_____

Now that we have you on the path to being loosely organised, we are going to start to explore some interesting concepts about how to improve your positive energy levels, and therefore the outcome of each day.

The old computer acronym G.I.G.O. stands for Garbage In Garbage Out. Meaning if you put rubbish into a computer, then you will only get rubbish out. The higher the quality of bits and bytes put into the computer, whether at the programming level or at the user level, then of course the higher the quality data you will get back from your computer.

I know we are not computers, but computers are based on human brain functionality. How can they not be, they are designed by human brains - to operate like a super fast brain.

Our brains have a similar problem to computers; the more junk we feed into our brains, the less the quality of the work done within them – the thinking.

One of the very vulnerable times for our brains, is just before we retire at night. If we feed our stomachs a meal of fat enriched donuts just before bed, we do not sleep so well because our body is speeding up to deal with the processing of fats and sugars, the same applies to coffee. The same also applies to our brain, and as the food of the brain is thoughts and action generated ideas, and then we must take care of the input quality.

If you watch something like Amityville Horror, or even the late night news, turn off your television and go to sleep you will not sleep restfully. We know in our conscious mind that it is just a movie, but the subconscious mind is busy. It does not know the difference between reality and a DVD, that is why we can feel emotion in a movie like fear, or sadness or even happiness. That is why a movie with a good ending makes us feel good.

If you argue with someone and go to sleep angry, your sleep pattern will be disturbed and you will awake feeling unrefreshed and tired.

The last 30 minutes before sleeping should be a steady wind down into a relaxed and restful mode. Play soft music, read or watch something uplifting or relaxing, or even neutral like a National Geographic wildlife program (not Seconds from Disaster!). Sit outside on a summer evening, walk your dog, tell someone you love them, prepare for tomorrow – but ensure all the final input is quality, positive and restful. Then when you finally close your eyes, your mind is ready to relax and give you good, sound restful sleep.

Lighting is also important, try to spend the last hour at least in lowered lighting, not under bright fluoro. Our bodies naturally wind down as the sun sets, but we recreate the light aspect and create false daylight in modern lifestyles. We use a lot of candles every evening, for aromatherapy and tranquil ambience of a flame.

Watch every day for excessive amounts of negative input coming your way and try to deflect, or at least minimise the personal impact. This means what we choose to watch, to listen to, to experience. Protect yourself against negative energy.

Tomorrow we will look at ways to do this, in the meantime – what's on your agenda tomorrow? and are you ready?

My Notes

Day 10   *Deflect the Negative Rays!*

I hope you slept well, and awakened to a glorious new day with renewed energy.

We are going to look at ways to deflect inbound negative energy in abnormal amounts – well actually any inbound negative energy, but let's tackle the biggies first.

There are two kinds of negative events in life, those we can do something about and those we cannot.

We can do something about negative people in our lives; we cannot stop bad people doing nasty things to others. We can however, minimise our chances of being the victim of a person with bad intentions.

We can change situations we are in, by truly changing them (e.g. leaving a situation) or by reframing them. Both work to assist us in deflecting negative impact.

Let us take a look at a very powerful tool, you can access from within. Reframing.

It is the ability to view things differently. In The Little Red Success Book, I give the example of a friend who had a kitchen window overlooking her garden. It was such a lovely view, I wondered why it was partly obscured by curtains. When I moved the curtains, I realised they were her clever way of reframing something negative. She lived in an industrial area, and could not relocate for personal reasons. Her window overlooked smokestacks and high tension wires of an industrial estate, dirty ugly and negative. However, by cleverly draping the window in a nice fabric, she created had instead a view of beauty and elegance. Her small terraced garden and fountain. The industrial estate was no longer there when one looked out the window.

We can use reframing for almost every situation. It can be mental and/or physical. If you have someone that you want to be near, who is constantly negative towards you, you can reframe that person. Understand why you want them to be near, understand that the negativity is their problem and not yours. No longer hear it, or respond to it. If you focus on the positive reason why you want this person in your life, and coach them gently on being more positive, you will be surprised that you feel less aggrieved about their attitude. You will minimise the negative impact!

Apart from reframing, you can take time out. Excuse yourself from a negative situation. Go someplace quiet and regroup your thoughts into a positive wall of protection. When you reface the negativity it will seem smaller. You can use the 'bubble' technique. Mentally place yourself inside a transparent bubble, where all is well in your world, do not allow anyone negative inside your bubble. This can be a good short term solution.

Tomorrow we will look at how to minimise the impact of negative events.

My Notes

Have you tried reframing anything, or anyone yet? It can even be fun.

Today I want to help with what to do to ease the pain of negative events. These are often things that we had no control over, but they can control us – our emotions, our situation, they can be all consuming.

We cannot control what happens to us, we can only control our reactions. We can also minimise our chances of being involved in some negative events such as a victim of a scam, mugging or theft. We cannot completely prevent it, but we can help.

Our reactions will dictate what happens to our brains, and our bodies, in the event of a crisis, or negative event. Our reactions will often ignite, or calm, those around us as well. We can control our reactions to almost every situation.

First and foremost, we must try and remain as calm as possible in any event. Screaming, anger, yelling, crying, pleading, or other displays of negative emotion are not as powerful as a calm, rational voice.

When we generate a large amount of negative energy, our bodies release large doses adrenalin – the fight or flight hormone. Adrenalin clouds our brains ability to think rationally. The person who is mentally in control will be the strongest, and the most likely to win an argument, talk their way out of a bad situation, or help those around them. The one who will be in mental control is the calmest person. Even psychopaths can increase their energy by feeding from the energy of their victims.

Whatever life deals out to us, is in the end likely going to add to our strength or cause us to drop the ball and fall behind. We cannot change the event, be it a death, divorce, fire, natural disaster, illness or attack. We can however increase our strength to cope better and recover faster. You know this, you see how some people come out as a powerhouse after disaster strikes, and these are the ones who know how to react in the best way.

When the hand of life deals you a bad hand, try to remember that only YOU are in control of your actions. Only YOU can decide what the future will be for you. Do not allow others to judge you for how you choose to react, remember most people are not that happy or successful, and they behave in a collective tribal sort of way. Thus pressure and expectation is on you to do the same. Listen only to your own heart and mind, and react in a way that minimises your downtime and the impact on your future. Be just a little selfish and do not let others or events drain all your energy.

It has worked for me through death, divorce, financial crisis, redundancy and friendship issues. It will work for you too.

My Notes

_____

_____

_____

_____

_____

_____

_____

_____

_____

_____

Some days we have to face negative situations at work, at home, in life generally.

The most important thing to understand is remaining centered. This is a state of mind where you feel grounded, connected to the earth. It helps you be clam, rational and authoritative thus increasing your personal power.

When you know you have to handle a negative situation, you have to consider the best way to do so. Where possible avoid putting your personal energy in the space. By this I mean, if a lawyer can handle it for you that is better, if someone else that you trust can be your emissary that's a good thing. You can preserve and protect your personal energy bank from the debits of runaway emotions.

However, some things must be faced personally for various reasons. When this happens, if you first visualise how you would like it to go that is a great start and forms a map for the energy to follow.

Once you are a few minutes from facing the situation, take some time out (even use the toilet) to breathe slowly and deeply, and put your mind into a state of complete calm. Feel the ground beneath your feet; understand that whatever the outcome, you will actually be ok. This is centering. Sometimes in strange ways it is even better afterwards, because you are stronger. Even if you are broke as an outcome, life will re-establish itself and you can still recover and be happy. If you are ill, at least you will have confirmation of what is wrong, and can go about deciding on your choice of treatment.

However, if you visualise strongly enough in a negative situation where you can influence the outcome, maybe you will be amazed at your own power to create a positive outcome. Help may come from unexpected sources. When you are centred, you are like a huge pillar, self supporting and withstanding generations of weathering.

Focus on words like calm, rational, powerful, clarity, and if at all possible, stand with the sun on your face for a few moments and really feel the power that is available to you to use.

Power is strongest in calm, rational states of mind. Power then becomes like a scalpel – focussed, incisive, unwavering and unable to be shaken by emotive attacks from others.

My Notes

We have looked at some pretty amazing stuff over the past twelve days.

We have explored the use of planning each day to maximise your use of energy, success and time for fun.

We asked you to have a look at your image and see if that reflected the sort of person who should get what you want.

We have made a plan of the top 10 things you want to achieve this year, and filed it away in a safe place to check on the same time next year. This is going to be a very exciting day for you, when you really know what is possible!

Then we started looking at how much time we all waste looking for things, sorting out the consequences of bills we forgot to pay, or missed appointments. Here we see you can have lots of extra time available for fun, study or whatever makes you happy.

We spent some time sorting out the junk, and getting rid of it.

Then we have looked at some simple practices to minimise the effect of negative people and situations.

If you didn't do anything in any of these simple exercises, yet you really want to feel happy and be successful, then I suggest you go back and start again.

If you got behind, understandable, as there is a lot going on here each day......just slow down the pace of reading, the next pages will wait for you ☺

If you followed each day's recommendations, then you are well on your way to a more organised life that allows more room for impulsive fun. A life that has more time for happiness and you will spend less time stressing out. That is a more balanced life that we all deserve.

Over the next few days we are going to look briefly at how to use affirmations and visualisation, appreciation and the importance of commitment to your ideas and goals.

If you are enjoying your results so far, then maybe you can think about also reading The LITTLE RED SUCCESS BOOK, which has a 7 step program to explore some of these steps a bit further.

Meanwhile, spend a few minutes thinking about the last few days and preparing for the first day of the rest of your life – it is just tomorrow!

My Notes

You will hear a lot about visualisation in the self help industry, and yes it is an industry – a service industry.

Does visualisation really work? YES, it sure does. It is another powerful tool, like centering, that can really change your life.

If you really want a goal, then you need to be able to alert as many of your senses as possible. We all believe what we see! Therefore being able to see, in our mind, what we want clearly - is a very powerful attractor.

Ideally start with a visual picture in your mind, or from a photograph or drawing that represents it. When you focus on this picture, you will eventually start to be able to hear it, and even smell it. As each sense is alerted and engages, the vision becomes more powerful and you will get a very positive spiral effect.

Let us say you really want a beautiful motorbike, like I did. I had a picture of the bike I wanted on my desktop every day. I had to take lessons, and get a full license to ride. So as I made my plan, visualisation became the thing that kept my dream alive. When I fell off during my lessons, I was able to get back up because by then I could see and smell, and even hear in my mind the roar of my new bike ☺

Whatever you want can be visualised. It is not however possible to visualise another person in your picture, as they may have a different dream. When energies conflict they form a whirlpool and just absorb energy but go nowhere.

If you are seeking a new partner, do not visualise the person down the street, or in the office. Visualise instead the type of person you want to be with, how they would treat you, what you would do together. Or just simply visualise yourself living in harmony with someone else, focus on how you would feel.

New material objects, money, and things like houses are an easy visualisation. It is easy to visualise your bank account, a nice home or a new coat! It is not wrong to want visual objects, but don't expect them to make you happy in themselves. They cannot, they are inanimate objects! I have heard some mentors say that it is wrong to want money, but of course it isn't! The fields of energy do not have emotions and judgement, the law of attraction just works without judgement and censorship.

Spend some time today visualising the things you wrote in your top 10 goals for this year, fix these pictures clearly in your mind, and refer to them when you need something to strive for.

My Notes

Affirmations really work. I know they sound a bit alternative and new age, but they really do work.

Think of them as subconscious mind training instead. They work exactly the same way as when you want your dog to fetch a ball! Repeated often enough, rewarded when right, the ball is delivered with increasing regularity until 100% is achieved.

Affirmations are the same. You can use affirmations to get your subconscious mind, (who is always busy, but often up to mischief), focussed on achieving what you want. You can use them to help your mind to heal your body of illness and complaints. They are so easy to use, that most people stop using them – it is too good to be true!

They will change how you react to situations, they will bring to you energy from unexpected places, they will simply make you feel better.

This is a big topic, and we only have one day, so let's cut to some fast tracking.

If you are ill, or in pain, I recommend you buy Louise Hay's 'Heal Your Body' You can buy it online from www.terrieanderson.com or your favourite bookstore. It is my main healing book. Whenever I have pain, or feel ill, I go straight to that complaint in her list and use the affirmations. It usually clears even a chronic issue after just a few days! Drug Free! If this was the only thing you gained out of these 30 days, you are already a winner!

An affirmation should be said or read aloud 3 times, at 3 times per day until no longer needed.

I have short term affirmations for things I need to create or change soon, long term affirmations to maintain my mental health and then I use them to affirm my goals. It works!

My small gift to you today is to try an affirmation for yourself:

'I am happy and successful. I am healthy and wealthy. I am free'

Take note of how you feel today. Say this aloud 3 times x 3 times every day. After one week you will notice the difference in how you feel. At the end of week two, you will notice you had a much better week!

Enjoy, and then make your own to use that are meaningful just to you.

My Notes

Day 16　　　*Appreciation is A Secret Weapon*

To receive more than we have at any moment in time, we should be able to express appreciation for everything we have in our lives today.

Even the food on our table every evening, no matter how rich you are today, something may take it all away and you would experience having no food, so be appreciative of what you have.

Appreciate the qualities you are given, your ability to communicate, the legs that carry you, the hands that work for you, and the mind that makes everything possible.

If you are just a normal, able bodied person with an average intelligence – you already have a huge advantage over many. Appreciate this advantage.

This doesn't mean thanking your God, or spending hours in appreciation, but it can be a dynamic thought process. As you walk around your house notice small things, and silently enjoy them! Look about your office and see a colleague you admire, and silently contemplate what they have taught you. When next you see a parent, or think of a parent, remember some of the nice things they did for you. Smile often as you do this, a quiet inside smile on your soul. If you see 50cents on the ground, pick it up, put it in your pocket and appreciate you just received unexpected wealth. Do not walk over it with contempt as it is too small, every million dollars can be reduced to a pile of 50 cent pieces!

If you are having a sad or bad day – think of someone you really like, and mentally appreciate them.

Now it is additionally powerful, if you always remember to say Thank You for everything thing, or service, you receive. It only takes a second, but it is measured in positive inputs to your world. Try to actually mean it, look at the waiter who brought your drink for a second and say Thank You to them, not under your breath or as an aside.

If you live in a state of appreciation, it makes you a person to be appreciated. Many small gifts of appreciation will come your way, like upgrades without asking, free bonuses, and extra discount will just surprise you. People will be nicer, actually it is a mirror and your attitude is reflected.

This is a rewarding two way street, everything you give out comes back multiplied many times. Now I am not talking about charity here, just small random acts of kindness and remembering to say Thank You. You would be shocked to observe how many people, do not bother! This will change the outcome of your days!

My Notes

Day 17   Commitment

In our office we have a framed quotation from Goethe. I am going to quote this here for you. We all think it encapsulates how commitment works.

UNTIL ONE IS COMMITTED, THERE IS THE CHANCE TO DRAWBACK, ALWAYS INEFFECTIVENESS.

CONCERNING ALL ACTS OF INITIATIVE (AND CREATION) THERE IS ONE ELEMENTARY TRUTH, THE IGNORANCE OF WHICH KILLS COUNTLESS IDEAS AND SPLENDID PLANS

- THE MOMENT ONE COMMITS ONESELF, THEN PROVIDENCE MOVES TOO

ALL SORTS OF THINGS OCCUR TO HELP ONE, THAT WOULDN'T HAVE OTHERWISE OCCURRED, A WHOLE STREAM OF EVENTS ISSUE FROM THE DECISION, RAISING IN ONES' FAVOUR ALL MANNER OF UNFORESEEN INCIDENTS, MEETINGS AND MATERIAL ASSISTANCE WHICH NO MAN COULD HAVE DREAMED WOULD COME HIS WAY.

BOLDNESS HAS GENIUS, MAGIC AND POWER IN IT.

-GOETHE

This clearly demonstrates the defined link between commitment and the Law of Attraction. It also amplifies some of the ideas that we have explored in the past 17 days. For Universal energy to help you, you must know who you are and what you want! You need to be ready to receive what you want and believe you deserve it. Commit to what you want, and do not drop a dream because it's a bit hard. This is why I asked you to write down your top 10 goals for the year, writing them down is a strong form of commitment.

If something eventuates without any form of commitment, then I would class that as just good luck. Some people have an abundance of luck, some not much. I am one of the latter, I imagine and then create what I have, it does not just fall in my lap.

Commitment really creates focus, and focus is like a laser light, it fully engages the law of attraction on exactly what you want.

My Notes

Today, we are looking at eliminating and managing everyday fears and concerns that are not an immediate danger to anyone. To understand and accept fear, we must first embrace the concept that we experience fear because we are in our ego.

Most fear, or fear disguised and justified as "worry" will never actualise, it just will not happen.

If the feared outcome does happen then it will happen. It is what it is! There is little you can do to change the outcome, unless the fear is about your personal safety, or health, and you have been remiss in taking appropriate steps to alleviate the risk.

Understand that fear is mostly thoughts of the unknown, or possible consequences or events that may, or may not, ever take place. Once an event actually occurs, that fear is usually no longer present. If fear is present after the feared event has occurred, it is further thoughts of the unknown or possible further related events, in other words new fears.

Accept that these are only thoughts, fear is not usually reality. Learn to control these thoughts with unemotional detachment.

Reflection is an important tool to achieve this detachment. Take your fears, imagine them to be a small movie and play them through to their possible conclusions. Now you will be able to see what the fear really looks like, and you can begin to take control of yourself and your thoughts by also seeing how you would face this situation if it occurred. This will become easier to do with practise.

Write down a plan of what you would do in the event your fear occurred. Once you have a plan, you will feel more in control.

A common fear is flying. If you are afraid of flying, the reality is fear of crashing, injury and death - not a fear of flying! It is the same with every fear; it is just thoughts of a possible negative outcome or event.

Meditation will help remove the fear of death. As that is most often the ultimate fear, this will aid the control of many other fears.

One last comment here - The more you fear something, the more likely you will be using negative power to create the very thing you fear!

Even in very dangerous situations, the more you can hide your fear and appear calm the less you will agitate your predator, they often feed on the energy from your fear. A calm rational approach may mean you are able to leave the situation unhurt.

Fear, especially harbouring everyday fears, is a damaging and draining emotion. It will prevent you from achieving everything you want to be, it will stop you being happy.

The important thing is that you can overcome your fears, and celebrate life today!

My Notes

Are you planning your days? If you are, you should be noticing by now, that's a lot of daily goals you are achieving. It doesn't have to be 100% to be successful; it just has to be better than before and improving!

If not, you are still here – so why not give it a go? Surprise and amaze yourself at what you can do.

Let's have a quick look at guilt; it is a very heavy load for anyone to carry. It will certainly prevent you from achieving everything you want, and from being very happy, because guilt has a nasty habit of making us feel unworthy. 'I do not deserve to be happy' because you did something wrong – or think you did.

When we looked at confidence and image, self esteem on Day 2 – did you see a person burdened by guilt?

If you have a reasonably healthy body – do you stand up straight and look people directly in the eye? Or do you allow your shoulders to sag, your spine to bend forward or prefer to look away? The answer to these questions will tell you lots about how heavy your bag of rocks is. Symbolically our bodies respond to a weight on our mind, and guilt is a very heavy weight. It does no-one any good!

Look at what you feel guilty about, and take steps to remove the guilt. If you need to apologize to someone, go ahead and do so. Then move on. If that person is dead, you can leave a note on their gravesite, for example, to 'publicly' apologize.

If you need to right a wrong, then find a way to do it. You can resolve with the person you wronged, or to a child of theirs, or even to someone else in need. Example if you stole $100 from someone, but you can no longer find them – then give the $100 to a charity, or person, that needs it and that you think the wronged person would agree with.

If you lied to, or cheated someone and you cannot resolve it with them directly, you could use it as an example to teach others not to do the same. Or give some personal time to help someone, to balance the scales of energy again.

Above all, once you have taken a remedial action, and then let the guilt go and move on with your life – you owe no more, you can do no more!

Free yourself from guilt and learn to fly high and get what you want from life, you will feel freer and happier than ever before.

My Notes

Life's mosquitoes are all the little bugs that occur every day to distract and annoy us. There is a great expression that I refer to often 'Don't Sweat the Small Stuff' I do not know who originally said it, but it is even the title of a book by Richard Carlson, PhD, and also many articles.

If you truly want a happier life, then do not worry or get annoyed about the myriad of small annoyances that lie there in wait for us every day.

The bus is late. Your watch is slow. The toothpaste is squeezed from the top. The person next to you in the movies is a leg jiggler. Bad Manners. People ignoring my rights on the road. People honking their horn. Inconsiderate drivers like tailgaters. Kids not cleaning up their mess. Receiving chain emails. Someone playing music you do not like. People who promise and then do not deliver. Commercial breaks at critical points in a movie. People throwing cigarette butts on the ground. The sound of chainsaws.

All those small things listed above are just a tiny example of what bugs people. We are all different but we get bugged pretty easily, and that negative injection can turn a whole day into crap! I have seen relationships break over stupid, small things for people who otherwise were really cool together – what a shame!

Imagine - we can move away from that.

And, it is even EASY to do so!

IF you can change the bug, change it! (I.e. fix your watch now)

If you cannot change the bug, then STOP before getting annoyed; ask yourself 'How important is this?' 'Will I remember this tomorrow? ... Next month? ... next year?' Chances are you will not even remember it tomorrow, let alone next week. We easily remember the important things in life, but have you ever heard anyone say 'The keys were left on the wrong cupboard 11 times last year?' Yet, you may have quite cross about the keys being on the wrong cupboard, possibly caused ill feeling at home, started your day feeling negative, all over something you don't even recall later! What a waste of energy!

So, next time something small irritates you, stop and ask:

Can I Fix This? Yes, and then fix it! No, then keep going.....

Will I remember this tomorrow?

Will I remember it next week?

Will I remember it next year? If you answer this yes, then it is not a mosquito!

Then take a deep breath, and realign your position, realize and admit it's not worth an argument or a bad day.

My Notes

_____

_____

_____

_____

_____

_____

_____

_____

_____

_____

How is your daily planning going? Are you feeling a bit less stressed, a bit more in control of your life? If you have done what we discussed, then you will be. Congratulations.

Now, we are going to explore some more positive concepts.

Are you good socially? Or Are you Lonely? Do you want to connect with more people?

If you find it hard to go out and meet new people, the internet has opened a whole new world. I am a very outgoing and social person, but I also have grown to love my social networking, as I spend hours every day behind my computer and not with colleagues, so my friends can connect easily with me.

Start with Social Networking, whatever your situation is. You can spend as little as a few minutes a week, or as much as a few hours, it is up to you. Join at least Facebook and Twitter, plus LinkedIn if you are a business person or professional.

The benefits include:

People you have not heard from in years can easily find you and they do!

This has been a very positive experience for me, as many a boring kind of day has been brightened by an email from someone from years ago. The fact that they cared about you enough to find you, is such a buzz!

You meet lots of new people with similar interests and can express and share ideas, support causes, become involved in interesting debates or concepts.

You can give and receive advice and help from complete strangers who have knowledge you need, or recommendations and introductions to people who will matter to you.

PLUS – It just puts you out there and builds self confidence!

There are many negatives associated with the internet, but social networking is a revolution in reconnecting people with people, in the virtual world without the difficulties associated with the physical world.

Enrol today for at least one social network, and for goodness sake, put a real picture on – it makes a HUGE difference in your results! People want to know who they are talking to!

You can have lots of fun with this!

My Notes

_____

_____

_____

_____

_____

_____

_____

_____

_____

_____

I want to tell you about the most amazing man I have ever met. A true teacher of the law of abundance and attraction, although he probably didn't know it.

He was a salesperson, he was an immigrant to the country where he worked, and he was the most truly connected man I have ever known.

He worked for me as a sales person and had fantastic results every time. He was always smiling and genuinely happy. I was privileged to learn much about success from him.

If you walked in the street with this man, he knew almost everyone and more importantly they knew and acknowledged him! He had easy access to the highest levels of people in government, politics, corporations and societies.

How did he do this? Well, I wondered too, so one day I asked him for his secret.

This is what he told me:

It is simple. I just give every person I meet *One Minute More* and I remember to thank every person for everything they do for me, every time without fail. And??? That was it.

So, I closely observed him over the coming weeks. He did what he said, 100% of the time. Every person he encountered, he would transact his business, but he would take one minute more to make a personal connection. He did not stop strangers in the street or anything unsuitable like that, just everyone he dealt with in any way. The carpark attendant, the sandwich shop, the receptionists, the airline staff, the hotel staff, the waiters, clients, managers, CEOs, everyone!

People responded 95% of the time very positively.

How did he do it? He would ask them how their day was; he would comment on a nice smile, he would ask a question about their job – so easy, but so powerful. They remembered him.

Why did it matter? First he had a better day, and gave something positive to someone else. Second he had lots of positive energy credits. Third he got lots of gifts in return – upgrades, discounts, extra sandwich fillings, and Last but far from least he explained – these people also have sons, daughters, sisters, and parents. Some of those relationships were with people in very powerful positions and they would provide introductions at a social level which were very meaningful.

Everyone was in a win/win position, he always paid something to get something he wanted – a huge network.

I have used his advice, and it is amazing what happens and how your life changes. People will really help you every day.

My Notes

Three weeks into this new way of living, and we have looked at a lot of elements. How are you going?

Don't forget at any point, you can hit your PAUSE button, and resume again when you catch up. This is pretty heady stuff; if you take the actions it WILL have a positive impact on your life!

Think back over your last 22 daily plans, are your days a bit easier being better planned? Are you achieving more of your daily goals? By now, they should even be becoming less effort.

Are you handling some negative situations just a bit better? Keep practicing, because you don't want to stop now. You can have amazing results, so don't settle for average, or good enough. That would be undervaluing what you deserve.

Today, I want you to have a break except for tomorrows plan.

I want you to take the time you planned for today's exercise and go do something you really enjoy.

Call a friend for a chat, go for a run, walk the dog, watch a movie.

Revel in the pleasure.

You have now some time aside every day for this exercise, so you have already gained at least a few hours this month for yourself.

 Congratulations!

Now, Go and Enjoy Yourself! You deserve it!

My Notes

OK, today we are back to work on the 30 Days of Inspiration plan.

I have a question for you? Are you in debt? I do not mean a credit card account that you pay in full each month or a house payment you can easily afford, or commercial debt that is easy to service and works for your business. I mean personal debt. Personal loans, credit cards that are not paid in full each month, bills that are overdue, house payments too large – I think we know what I mean. And if you have business debt that is not easily serviceable it also enters this category.

Debt creates unhealthy stress levels, disturbs sleep, and generally messes with your head. How can you enjoy a beautiful sunset, glass of wine in your hand with your best friend if your debt levels are hard to service and they keep interrupting your peace!

So, if you are not in debt – congratulate yourself and stay that way! You are indeed fortunate, and have a head start. If you have no debt, maybe you can use this day for one of the other days' steps that you didn't finish.

For most of you, who are under some burden of debt – make a plan, right now.

First establish your current position. How much debt do you have, and do not cheat yourself. Then write a promise to yourself that you will not, except in dire emergency, use any more credit until you are debt free! Do not carry credit cards with you, except maybe one for emergency. This helps stop impulsive purchases.

Next draw up a budget for your monthly, or weekly expenses, including paying the debts.

You can progress quickly if your monthly income well exceeds your service of the debt, so let's look at what you need to do first.

You must act, even if your debt is easy to service, you never know what life holds – so better that you have no debt as soon as possible. Particularly credit cards have a nasty way of taking over your life, especially if you only pay minimum payments.

Look at your list, are there any overdue payments – make a plan to get rid of them first. You can usually make arrangements if you call your creditor. Then look at the smaller ones first, make a plan to get rid of them. Even if you pay an extra 10 dollars per week off one debt, you will be surprised how quickly it will reduce.

Lastly, you need to tackle the big ones, the same way - increase your payments on one debt at a time, by just doing without something else.

Your plan should be drawn up now for all your debts. First ensure you pay at least the required amount on every bill so it does not get behind, then select which order you wish to pay them off and how much you can afford to add to that debt until it's gone.

Why one at a time? Because it reduces faster, and this gives you encouragement and a sense of joy when one is gone! Celebrate!

For those of you whose debt repayment exceeds your income, you must start the same way. Make up your list, STOP spending on the cards immediately, and see what you can pay each month by order of essential services such as heating, energy, health, food and your housing needs. Then see what you need to service your debts.

Next look at where you can change things to save money. Can you use energy saving tips to lower energy costs? Can you downsize your house? Can you move to a less expensive town? What about your grocery bill, there is usually saving there – a big tip, is shop each day for just what you need that day. Do this on the way home and you can save hundreds of dollars in a month! Are your children or family members expecting too much? Can you sell anything that you do not use anymore?

Now, select the debts that are outside your budget, you just do not have funds each month to pay them. You will need to call your creditor/s and make an arrangement with them. Sometimes a creditor will accept a very small payment each month, until you have managed your overall position. Some will even accept a voluntary settlement rather than the cost of pushing you into bankruptcy or collection.

Facing any difficult debt, and putting in place a plan to recover, is the best way to come up with a plan to get out of a seemingly impossible situation. There are some situations where you are better to voluntarily settle for bankruptcy if there is no alternative, although this does have some long term effects on your life.

Above all, remember some people kill themselves deliberately, or through stress, about debt – it is not that critical. Debt is not a reason to dive into desperation, not ever, it is just debt. However you must manage it, thus a plan.

Most people can get out of debt by using the above techniques, but if your situation appears hopeless do not panic, the most important step is facing it and you have done that. There is always a way out that will restore peace to your life. People will help you to sort it out, there are even free counselling services or ask at your bank for help. Never despair, just make a peace plan for yourself!

Debt is one of the number one stress factors in modern life, yet it is not a survival thing – it is not about finding water or food for today's meal – it is something we have the power to change!

My Notes

After such a big exercise for some of you yesterday, you may not be feeling like a lot today, so it is going to be an easier step.

If you are one of the people with a big debt burden, then I recommend that you continue to work on that until you have a manageable plan, and just let the next few days steps wait until you are ready.

It is very easy when we sit with family and friends to spend time discussing others. Usually, sadly it is what is seen as the negative aspects of others, rarely do we see a group of people discussing the successes of all their friends. For some reason, I can never fathom, the average human interest seems to be in the negative. I think we are all programmed by the news!

If you want to be successful stay focussed on your path, your plans and your development. If you want to be happy celebrate the success of others, and leave the weaknesses for others to discuss.

Walk In Your Own Shoes!

Judgement generally makes us very unhappy and serves as a distraction (and sometimes an excuse) from our real purpose in life.

We do not ever understand all the facets of any individual other than ourselves (and even sometimes understanding ourselves can be challenging!) If we discuss what she wore, or that he gained weight, or that they went on holiday when they should have been someplace else (in our opinion) then we are trying to walk in their shoes!

Each person is a complicated cocktail of emotions, physical characteristics, mental states, stresses, and situations even occasionally abuse of self, or from others. We are manipulated and controlled by others, and when we discuss someone else we do not know all these factors. We do not know their IQ, education, social upbringing, personal circumstances, medication, or needs. Yet we will sit, like birds of prey circling their victim, and judge their actions. Usually these actions, are completely unrelated to us and do not directly affect us. (He left his wife, she wore bright colours to a funeral, they got drunk at a part, they bought this or that when you believe they could not afford it)

Next time you are with a group of friends or colleagues who are hell bent on discussing the negatives, or misfortunes, of others – then try changing the subject, or introducing a positive aspect. Stay well away from discrimination topics in general. If that fails, then 'Go sailing' in your head.

I am a sailor, and that's what I do when I do not want to partake in negative (and boring) conversation. I go sailing in my head, and if asked my opinion sometimes I have to apologise and say 'Oh, I am sorry I was drifting off' with a smile.

Every time you engage in a negative discussion about someone else – you actually transfer energy to that person! So instead, save that energy for your goals and plans. However, the reverse works, if you speak well of someone in return you will receive a small boost in energy. The more positive your conversations, the more positive your thoughts, the more a song floats in your head instead of a complaint!

Positive energy feeds positive energy, every time. Conversely negative energy does the same. There is also a multiplier effect, so the more of either one you generate, the more you receive.

From today forward, pledge to yourself to walk in your own shoes!

You will slip from time to time as we are changing a lifetime of habits here, so do not worry just remind yourself whose shoes you are wearing when you slip.

My Notes

I hope your daily plans for tomorrow are still happening; this should become a life time habit.

I have a small spreadsheet printed out on my desk, a page for every week and the following one. That is where my daily plans go for all the small stuff, and then I add the things from my diary. If I didn't meet one of my daily goals, I transfer it to the next day. It is a simple way to track your plans. I do still plan every night my following day, even if only to plan tomorrow will be a casual, spontaneous day without a plan!

Much of what you have learnt in the past 25 days will be affecting others. Most particularly the family members, or friends, who live with you. Today, I ask you to think about any effects that your changes may have on them and if any explanation is necessary.

Perhaps, for example, you decided that your children were going to have to have a little less treats so you can manage a debt. It is worthwhile to explain to them why you are taking this step, because it is a chance for them to learn too. It helps prevent, or at least minimise, arguments from them when you have to say no.

Perhaps you need to explain the new formula for finding things around the house, for example ' Could everyone please do me favour, and put the mail in the box on the cupboard each day, because I am trying to ensure things are better organised and it really helps me a lot'

Sometimes friends will want you to do things that you used to do, but you know now no longer fit your goals – so you will need to tell them that you are embarking on a new journey to reach your goals. They probably will not understand. It is human nature, for those of us without goals and plans, to want our friends to also stay the same. Difference and change alarms many people, but do not be afraid – these people if really your friends will understand. If they do not, then frankly, you will move on and develop new and more rewarding friendships.

Particularly, if you have a large group of friends that were all predominantly the same. Similar incomes, few goals, mostly negative and now you are going somewhere – they will want, (even for your protection) to keep you with them. You see it can be threatening if someone breaks rank, is more successful, happier - then it kind of exposes an excuse why all of them cannot do it. It makes people nervous!

Please do not worry, positive energy attracts more positive energy and new people will enter your life that have loftier ideals and goals too, and you will enter a new social sphere.

Parents and family can sometimes be the enemy of change and dreams, plans and goals! Sometimes they do not understand why you want to be different, achieve more, run a different race! So they will try and convince you not to take the risk for happiness and success. Remember, the choice is yours, today, tomorrow and forever!

Imagine if we taught young children what you have been learning in the past 30 days! Wouldn't that be just amazing! Children growing up with a happiness and success belief system. I do write articles for parents, teachers and children to try and change the way we mentally condition our kids.

My dream is to reach at least one million children with the message that they can plan to reach their dreams, no matter where they are today!

If you have children, talk them through the 30 Days with you. Teach them these principles and they can use them for a great head start in life. Be aware that if you have average teenagers, they may not listen today, but it does go in, and maybe they can come back to you later when they see the changes.

Particularly, we need to try and give our kids a positive message every day, hope for the future and an attitude of planning to succeed.

My Notes

Yesterday we looked at how the changes we are making will affect others, and sometimes the need to talk to them about what we are doing. I have a small additional piece of advice - do not openly share all your plans and goals freely. Share them only with trusted people who encourage you.

Many people will try and convince you that for you these goals are not possible. They cannot believe that someone with few prospects today could be tomorrow's political leader, millionaire, marathon runner, ideal father, make a lifestyle change, overcome disability or any other dreams you may have.

Again, I must remind you the choice is YOURS and only yours! You can do almost anything you want if you really want to, plan for it and follow the steps. Believe in yourself and be prepared to pay the price! (e.g. If you want an MBA that will mean less family time, if you want to run a marathon that will mean hard training).

Today, I want you to experience something very cool – positive energy response. I want you to do at least one random act of kindness for someone. Perhaps you buy a flower for an elderly lady that you know is lonely and just give it to her. Perhaps you help someone carry something, do a small task for someone who is stressed, give a waiter a special compliment about their service, even put some extra coins in a charity pot.

Feel what happens to you instantly, you will get a small buzz – an internal smile – a feeling that you are actually a good and deserving person. Once you learn to recognise and appreciate this feeling, you will find that doing small random acts of kindness regularly will boost your energy and make you smile more!

I have now a special gift for car drivers! If you have trouble parking, I would like you to try and amazing exercise that I cannot actually rationalise to you, but I know it is like magic.

Before you leave, just take a minute - close your eyes and book your car space where you want it. It must of course be a legal parking space. Imagine being able to drive up, and just park where you want. Yes, I know this sounds impossible - but just try it.

Before anyone on our team leaves, they always mentally book their space. You will be amazed how frequently just as you drive up someone leaves a space – it is yours. Or the space is waiting for you right at the door! We never have to park anywhere other than close by where we want to go, not ever! On rare occasions, we have to drive around the block at most twice! We were just a bit too early, or didn't give enough time. We ALWAYS park in a convenient space, close by!

This small exercise, if you truly do it, will amaze you. Tomorrow I will talk to you more about how you can use this very same practice for many things!

My Notes

If you are a car driver did you try booking your parking? Practice it regularly, until you become very confident with it! It truly works.

If you do not drive a car, you can try it on a restaurant table, a hairdresser place, or something similar.

The Law of Attraction works quite simply. Once we commit to a goal, in this case a very simple one (parking the car) try to imagine our energy reaches out and travels. Our subconscious mind is very connected to the energy that runs everything in the universe. It is exceedingly powerful, it can bring things to you that you confidently request and plan for. Always remember everything has a price, and we must be prepared to pay the price (not necessarily a cash price).

That energy, we commit to parking the car, goes out and causes a whole series of events to happen that would seem unimaginable. They do occur, and we attract to us the very thing we seek. In this case a car space. Sounds ridiculous – just try it a few times and see how it works!

I want to share with you a simple story.

A few years ago, I was having coffee with a senior executive friend of mine who is a very stressed person normally. We were discussing Christmas Shopping. I said I had gone to a particular shopping mall, that it was great, I parked my car near the door where I always park it – I went in and found the gifts I needed – I took them to the gift wrap bar – I went to the lovely Oyster Bar for a glass of champagne and rock oysters, seated at a nice table

– I collected all my beautifully wrapped gifts – left the mall and drove home.

She said ' Well you were lucky, I went to that mall too but I chose the worse day. I had to drive around 40 minutes to find a car park, and then I was 400m from the mall. I could only find two gifts, then the gift wrap bar was too busy, the Oyster Bar was full and I could not get a table, so I drove home so frustrated'

Imagine my surprise, when I discovered we were in the same mall, on the same day. We had arrived just ten minutes apart. Why the difference?

Well, I expected what I received – a nice, relaxed day enjoying the pleasure of selecting nice gifts for my friends and family.

She expected a huge hassle because it was Christmas time and everything would be stressed.

We each got what we planned for!

That is how the Law of Attraction actually works.

We get what we plan for, what we book, what we pay for – it does not discriminate between rich and poor, good and bad, it just delivers what we expect.

So from today onwards, try and retain that very simple secret in your mind. Plan for greatness, success, health, happiness and a wonderful life. If you plan for less, you will get less.

Then take action towards your goals and plans, always be honest with yourself and others. Give a fair deal for a fair price. Expect to receive the same and do not settle for less, and do not ask for more than a fair deal.

Radiate warmth and empathy towards people, listen to them when they speak to you, stay calm and in control. Plan, plan, plan and follow yourself up. Write down 10 goals a year. Have fun as much as possible, and do not do what others say is right, do what you believe is right. Your happiness is most important, you only have one life that we know of, don't waste it. Do not control the lives of others, but control your own and make your choices accepting responsibility. Live with confidence in yourself. Celebrate Your Life Every Day!

You are Amazing!

My Notes

Day 29   A Big Exercise – Coming Together

Now, we have spent 29 Days together. I hope you found it a rewarding experience. Even if you chose to do none of the exercises then you hopefully found some inspiration regardless. If you chose to do some of the exercises, then you will have made some significant positive changes in your life.

If you are one of the people who followed the program fully, by now you will have more free time to either have fun, or to dedicate to achieving your goals, or both together. You will be able to find things quickly, you will feel in control of your life and know where you are today, who you are today and where you want to go, who you want to be. You will have a plan to get there and you will be walking that path each day, actually knowing if what you did that day moved you closer or further away from your goals, and correcting your actions or adjusting your behaviour, when needed. If you needed help you will have either found it, or have a plan to seek that help.

You may be battling a few problem children around you, friends and family who want you to play safe and stay in your box. People who want you to be less successful and just go play with them like you did before, and they can share their miseries with you. These will fall away as you forge ahead with more and more power each day. You can be unstoppable!

Today, I want to bring some elements of the program together into one last big exercise.

First, do all the little things you need to do to set aside an hour for yourself.

Do tomorrows' plan and execute it. Clothes ready, briefcase or handbag set, car keys or bus ticket ready etc.

Now, your mind should be clear. I want you to sit comfortably and quietly and start to visualise what your life will be like when everything comes together. When you no longer need to search for things, you are a bit organised. When you no longer are restricted by debt or familial obligation, but instead what you do for your family is a joy.

On that day when it all comes together, maybe just a year or so from now, what will you look like? What will you be wearing? Imagine your face smiling in the mirror at the last minute check before you leave home.

Where will you live? What will your living environment look like? How much less debt will you have, or will you even have extra cash in the bank now?

When you leave the house on this day, how will you leave? Where will you be going? What job will you be doing? Will you be working from home?

Now, in your mind start to go about your ideal day and visualise how it will be in every small detail or aspect you can. Feel how you will feel on that day, look back and understand how worthwhile the hard work and changes you made were to get to this day.

Travel in your mind into your evening and what you will be doing, wearing, thinking and the type of friends you will spend it with.

You will have time to meet friends, your friends will be the kind of friends that match with who you are, and who you want to be.

You will be feeling good, more successful, and more self managed, more confident. You will attract the kind of people that you need in your life to help you go where you want to go.

Imagine you can manage your bills, you have enough to meet your needs, and you are no longer worrying you are 'on target'. You can find what you need to find quickly and easily, you buy what you really want and need and no extras because they were 'cheap'. You have less trash, as you shop for what you need regularly instead of binge shopping for food. (The once a week huge trolley is passé now.)

You have more time for your kids and can plan activities with them that you both enjoy; you can even inspire and motivate them too.

Spend about 20 mins doing this, you are using and practising many of the techniques we have gone through, all at once. You are strengthening your resolve, so I recommend doing this exercise when you feel a bit low, or over challenged, or at least once a month.

After this you will feel strengthened and remotivated towards achieving your goals.

Now, If possible, look in a mirror...... smile.....looks different huh? Then look again, this time thinking of something that makes you feel really good, and truly smile – wide – show your teeth – a big cheesy grin - WOW! - look at yourself! You are Amazing! How different is that look? (And feel).

Looks great, I want you to do this every night for the next week. Look in the mirror at yourself with a big cheesy grin. Do it at work if you have a bad day! It is a fast pep pill for the soul!

Ok, you are done now. Go and relax, enjoy yourself, you are on your way!

My Notes

_____

_____

_____

_____

_____

_____

_____

_____

_____

_____

I hope you have found the time we spent together was worthwhile, and that you are feeling happier, freer, in control of your life - or on the way. That you are starting to enjoy more free time previously spent being aggravated, irritated, bored, searching for a piece of paper, or having a problem with life's 'mosquitoes'.

I want to share with you something from my wall, that I read every day and remind myself about who I want to be!

It says:

LOOK FAMOUS

BE LEGENDARY

APPEAR COMPLEX

ACT EASY

RADIATE PRESENCE

TRAVEL LIGHT

SEEM A DREAM

PROVE REAL

This keeps me motivated and on track to fulfilling the destiny of the person I want to be.

Every day, I still keep up a cycle of doing the things we have discussed in the last 30 days, and I am delighted to share with you that after a few years like this, I still feel a sense of euphoria each and every day. Rarely does a days' activity or problems get on top of me for more than a few minutes. I am truly happy, ready for the next adventure and ready to take advantage of any opportunity that comes along with the right vision. I look forward to what each day brings, and the people I will meet, the food I will taste and I am very grateful to have received the knowledge of abundance and attraction, from others.

You too, can be happy and successful every day. You just have to want it enough to take the actions, and follow them through.

One last small gift – a trick to a better day – *Be careful what questions you ask. Do you really want or need to know the answer? Sometimes the answer irritates you even more, but maybe you didn't need to know.*

Let us say, someone who works for you did something silly. We are already possibly irritated, and then we usually ask 'Why?' I wonder why that is......what the hell does it matter why they did it? The answer will no doubt really challenge us and screw up a at least a small part of our day. We do not need to know why!

Just fix it and get on with your day.

When you are tempted to ask any question, just verify with yourself that you really 'need' to know the answer, and stay away from idle curiosity! If you do not need to know, stop mid tracks and do NOT ask that question. I promise you will have a better day, and when someone asks you 'why did they do it?... it is fun to say to others 'I don't know why, does it matter why?'

This next paragraph is very important:

I have seen many people start with this path, and it works SO WELL, they stop doing it. They get complacent; they think it was just a one of exercise. They forget that breaking many years of habits is not so easy, and that once you stop working at it, those habits quickly take control again. You can end up where you started, and then maybe think it didn't work!

Don't STOP!

I enjoyed our thirty days together, and I hope you did too!

Enjoy your own personal journey, and I hope one day we meet,

Terrie

My Notes

You have completed your guided transition into a new way of thinking, feeling and being. IF you did everything I asked you to, then you will feel much lighter and more in control of your life and your destiny. You will have hours more time every month to do the things you choose to do – don't waste this time – use it to have fun, meet connections or get ahead!

Remember, it is so important now, not to stop doing these things every day, week, month, year!

Make sure you have a daily plan, every day – it must be a habit or you will stop doing it. If you want to have an unplanned day – so be it – write 'free day' in your diary and enjoy it.

Don't get bitten by life's mosquitoes, or if you did, then apply a remedy quickly and forget the bite!

Remember to try and reframe negative input, and situations, that you choose not to escape.

Don't tolerate crap from the people around you anymore! You don't have to be rude, just block it out and go look in that mirror and remind yourself you are not only OK, you are actually amazing!

Be open and honest. Carry a warm smile. Whilst you want to be friendly, do not make friends or trust people too quickly. You can have hundreds of acquaintances that are nice to spend time with but you do not have to trust your safety to them.

Walk away from as much negativity as you can, and clear out of your mobile and your address book the names of people you really do not want in your life.

If you have things that bring back pain and sad memories, think about either getting rid of them or putting them in a far corner of the attic and forgetting them. Surround yourself with as much beauty and things that make you happy as you possibly can. Even if you are 'flat broke' you can take a walk in a field and bring home a nice flower, or some nice grasses for your table. Beauty can often be found for free, someone else's junk can be your art!

Spend time with people who make you feel good, help you to laugh more! Talk to strangers, just don't trust them instantly. Smile at everyone you can and wish them a 'Good Day'

Listen to music that makes you feel great, even as loudly as your neighbours will tolerate if you are alone. Turn off TV when someone visits you and actually share the time, in the moment with them.

Stop garbage coming IN your mind. Choose carefully what you allow to be input, especially near important events in your life.

Make sure you use that spare time that I have shown you how to find to do some really joyful things. Play a game with the kids ion your street, take a dog for a walk, go watch sunsets or sunrises – all the things that will release your mind.

Most people gain back at least an hour a day, and that is 30-31 hours a month, if they follow each of the actions in this guide. We just don't track how much time we waste looking for things, forgetting things, apologising because we forgot, rushing about at the last minute and screwing up events because we didn't organise ourselves!

You *are* Amazing – You Can Realise Your Goals – Everyone has huge potential for success and happiness.

Remember for some of you, the road is a very hard one due to disability, so for the rest of us who are at least average intelligence, healthy and fully able bodied – WOW! Nothing but ourselves holds us back!

A quick comment on money – There is plenty of money around! Maybe it isn't in your pocket right now, but you can have the money you need to succeed, it will come to you, but you must change how you think about it. If you keep thinking about money in a negative way, it never will. Billions flows around the globe every day, so it is out there. We just have to focus on getting our lives together in a lot of small ways and the money will start to increase in our pocket.

You know it is an economic paradigm that if all the money in the world were evenly distributed today, that within a very short time the money would all be back where it started. Those that know how to attract and generate wealth would continue to do so. The others would lose it, because they still have negative money beliefs, so it will leave them quickly.

Be just a little selfish and think about your life, your plans and needs. Love yourself first before you try to give anyone else love. Please get rid of any guilt you carry, and reduce those fears of anything, especially failure. You will then fly free!

Go Now and Enjoy Your Life to the Fullest!

Reach Out and Connect...

If We Can Communicate Effectively We Can Perform Miracles!

A Preview of Terrie's Next Book Due Early 2010

A lot of stress and angst can be removed from our lives if we can learn to effectively communicate.

Communication is far more than words; it involves body language, eye movement, contact and actions. In total silence it is possible to convey a message of aggression, love, anger, fear or intolerance.

Great communication is when the physical, mental and verbal activity is all in one state. When they are not there, it can be misread or confused messages, a shutdown of communication or an interpretation of dishonesty.

The best state of mind to communicate effectively is of course a calm state of mind, but we all know this is not always possible. However there are still ways to communicate, and actually connect, more effectively than most of us do today, even when stressed.

Great communication is always two way – even in a one way address – such as a guest speaker. We will look later at the concept of communicating with yourself, something most of us are actually not that good at! However, back to the point, it is still two way.

Even when you address an audience, you are actually speaking to each member of the audience in a two way communication between each person and you. If you are a great speaker, your audience will have no communication with anyone other than you, during the time allotted for your speaking. You are speaking to them, they are listening and trying to comprehend your message. The more interesting and relevant your message to them, the better will be the level of communication.

Members of your audience will communicate back to you, most likely silently with the use of body language, and attention, (even eye contact) how they are receiving your message. If they receive it well, you will note they are paying attention to you, nodding smiling and looking comfortable in their seats. If they are not happy, you will see restlessness, perhaps people leaving or talking to each other, looking around the room – in short not looking comfortable. This is a two way communication that many speakers miss.

When you are in a group conversation, similar interaction takes place. Next time you are waiting in a public place – a bus, a train station, a restaurant – take a look at the people having conversations around you. Observe the speaker and then their audience. Is their audience listening with interest? What is their body language? What messages are they sending to the speaker? How many people are sitting together, and not speaking or communicating at all?

From this simple art of observation, you will begin to understand the energy exchange that takes place between any two people engaged in communication. You will see easily, how well they are communicating, and whether they have connected or not. If we are not connected it is like talking to a telephone line that is not connected, a waste of breath as no one hears you.

So, now we have established that every communication is two way, we will look at some of the most common kinds of communication.

First, there are the personal interactions like a social or business greeting such as a handshake, kiss to the cheek, or wave across the room. Verbal interaction is another in this group and includes the greeting message, talking, listening and physical reactions. Then there is touch, which normally should be kept for close relationships such as parent and child, carers, friends, couples etc. Touch can offend people of some cultural backgrounds, and we need to be respectful of those who do not wish to be touched by people other than close family members.

Then, at the other end of the spectrum there is the non personal communication such as newspapers, magazines, television, radio and other media. Yes, even on those billboards someone is trying to reach out and connect with you! They have a message they want you to understand.

In the middle we have the personal, restricted communication, such as email, sms and letters. These are personal because it requires a physical and mental action on your part to send a message to someone, but restricted because that person can only use the visual sense to receive it. They cannot see or hear your mood or intent. So the message can go horribly wrong, because for example, you may send a happy joking message to someone who is having a sad or bad day, and they may misinterpret it.

Phones are a category of their own, because although not as good as face to face contact, most people are very familiar with the phone and can feel your mood along with hearing the words.

You can also express yourself much more clearly. There is less likelihood of accidental offence. However, for people like me, who are extraordinarily visual, and not so strong at auditory response, then the phone is still a challenge for excellent communication.

We are going to cover most of these methods of communication in the book, however our initial focus will be on face to face, personal communication. If we can get this well developed, then we are well on the way to adapting other forms of communication.

If we can communicate very effectively, we can perform miracles and achieve great things easily.

The most significant part of any communication is respect.

In all forms of communication, we must respect the person we are speaking to. Politeness, confidence and a smile will mostly attract a positive response. Now, some people are just rude, they would not bother to read this book, and from some of them you will still get a negative response, and this we must just brush away as a mosquito bite of life.

Respect is shown in simple ways. If you want to address a stranger, or passer-by, start with 'Excuse me' – this works in almost any language as a non-threatening opener.

What are you excusing yourself for? Most likely for interrupting them, and for taking their time and energy.

A soft smile is another good signal to a stranger that you do not have ill intent. Many people in today's life feel under threat. They read bad things in the newspapers, or see scary stories on television, and live in fear of being harmed by a stranger.

It is therefore your first task to show you are not a threat, and that you are humble, and respectful, about interrupting their day. After you address your subject, (for example you asked them for directions) thank them very much and wish them a good day. Even if they did not, or could not, help you this will mean you will be remembered in good stead, and you will receive a positive energy boost.

An example of a situation like this happened to me recently in Switzerland.

We were standing at a train station, when a young couple came and asked us quite bluntly for 2.50, for their train fare home. The truth was, as we were travelling through, we only had Euros in small change in our pockets. The Swiss currency is Swiss Francs.

I replied respectfully, 'I am sorry I only have Euros.' We were immediately abused and told to **** off. An unpleasant interchange, but it made us happy we had not had the opportunity to help those people.

Later, in the same evening, I was waiting at the corner for my partner to buy a burger, and another young couple approached. They were polite, and smiled, and explained they only had enough money for one burger and wondered if I could spare the change for a second one.

Again my answer was the same, I was sorry I only had Euros. They said they could not use the Euros but thanked me for my time, and for offering them the Euro. They wished me a nice evening.

It was very cold, and I just 'felt' these young people were genuine, so I went across the Street and found my partner, who by now had some Swiss Francs. I then went around the corner and found this young couple and gave them a little more than they asked for. They were so happy, and we were rewarded by seeing them rush into McDonalds and buy the two burgers and an ice cream each. They had happiness all across their faces and body language.

I am sure you can see the difference; I bothered to take extra action to help the second couple because they had connected with me in their communication. I believed them and appreciated their respect.

To make a strong verbal connection we must understand as much as possible about our audience. i.e. the other person, or people we want to connect with.

This is, of course, unnecessary for short interaction with strangers. A chance encounter such as an "excuse me" incident, or asking someone directions or the time, does not need you to understand your audience. However, an excellent communicator would ensure that the respect we discussed above is honoured.

It is much easier when we know our audience well, such as family members, friends, work colleagues with whom we interact on a daily basis etc. However, we also need to learn how to do some *30 second research* when we meet someone for the first time. If we really want to connect with them, and have our message understood. This is a great skill to have. Once practised, it becomes automatic and happens at a sub-conscious level.

If you are a sales person take note, this is very useful knowledge for you, if you want to enjoy success and repeat business

Operational Senses

Each person we meet has a mode in which they operate dominantly. There are three main senses we use to interact:

Visual Sense (Seeing)

Auditory Sense (Listening)

Kinaesthetic Sense (Feelings)

Most people use all three modes, in a variety of mixes per person, however each of us is usually dominant in one of the senses.

For example the colleague sitting next to me is probably around 50% visual, 30% auditory and 20% kinaesthetic. This means when I communicate with him, I use as many visual words as possible, draw pictures of what I mean both literally and figuratively, and talk things through usually repeating the message to reinforce it. I use less 'feeling' words. This way he hears my message, and sees my meaning quite clearly.

This is not so difficult, because I am also very visual.

However another colleague on my team is probably about 70% kinaesthetic, 20% visual and 10% auditory. This is kind of the opposite end, of the communication scale, from me. So I have to express everything a little differently when I speak to him.

He does not hear my message easily, and he does not see my meaning, he needs to 'feel' my meaning. This is difficult, because I am lower on the kinaesthetic scale, so I have to use a mode of communication in which I am weak. Some other team members get into conflict, or shut down, with this young man because they do not understand how to connect with him.

On every team, and in every family unit, and with every group of friends or colleagues there will be a lot of misunderstanding just because of this simple neurolinguistic programming. Often this misunderstanding can be silent, so no one is aware that one, or even a few, people got a completely different idea from what was said.

Sometimes two people can be arguing about the same thing, but neither can express their ideas in a way that is comprehensible to the other. This is due to the different communication modalities. This is a shame of course, as ill feelings and frustration can arise when there is no need, they are actually in agreement. They just do not recognise it.

When we meet someone, we need to listen very carefully to how they express themselves in the first few minutes. Listen for things they say that represent feelings, visual or auditory signals for their primary modality.

Do they say things like 'I feel' or 'I see'?

Where are they looking when they talk to you?

A visual person will have locked onto your eyes and face.

An auditory person will be focussed on listening and not hearing. They may be flicking their eyes around your facial perimeter, the ceiling, and the walls – they may notice what is happening around you, but still be very aware what you said.

A kinaesthetic person will be looking usually down, at the floor, the table, or a fixed space nearby your head – but rarely makes eye contact for more than a second or so.

When you shake hands, a visual person will probably make eye contact immediately.

An auditory person is likely to spend some seconds ensuring the hands connect, and then make shorter eye contact.

A kinaesthetic person may try and avoid your eyes altogether.

 The handshake itself should not be considered for this purpose, the type of handshake is affected by cultural background, customs, health and confidence.

If you have the chance to be in the physical space of the person, then look around:

What can you see to give you information for your quick research?

Is the space filled with interesting things? Visual people usually need things to look at to occupy their mind.

Is it filled with family photos? Kinaesthetic people like to have familiar warmth nearby.

Is it lacking a personal touch, or filled with gadgets?

For example; auditory people like phones, recording devices, speakers, music, and are less likely to notice bare walls.

None of this is foolproof, but my research over about 30 years, has demonstrated it is a fast, and reasonably accurate way to establish how best to connect with someone.

Now that you understand a little more about how to do your 30 second research, we need to explore how to use that information to effectively to make a good connection.

If you determine that your audience is visual, then you need to communicate with them in 'visual' terms.

This can be difficult if you are, for example, strongly kinaesthetic, but with practice you can.

I am very strongly visual, almost an extreme case, yet I have taught myself to communicate at all three levels. Now, I do not say that I am perfect at this, but every time my communication screws up, I know I missed the chance, because I did not take the time to communicate in the mode of my audience.

Once you have this knowledge, it is to your advantage to make use of it for effective communication. It is never the other party's responsibility; remember it is you that wishes to convey a message.

I have witnessed some amazing conversations between two people who both understand this concept, and they each speak in the language of their audience. This way both people are maximising their understanding of the other, and truly making a memorable connection.

We will look at ways to connect with each modality, however remember some people have a very even modality balance (e.g. 40% -30% -30%) so they will have influences of all three.

If you determine the primary modality of your audience is:

Kinaesthetic

With a kinaesthetic audience you need to limit eye contact, particularly for prolonged periods of time. Whilst we are often taught that eye contact shows honesty, and that is true, many 'feeling' people find it confrontational.

Some of the best scammers can look you right in the eye, as they remove your watch from your wrist!

Try sharing the same eye 'prop' that your audience uses. For Example: In business meetings this is often the table or desk; with kids, it is usually their shoes, your stomach or the table; and with someone at the bar - the bar and the glass will feature as props.

Express yourself in a feeling way. This audience needs to 'feel 'the meaning, as they have less focus on hearing and comprehending it, and may not be able to see it in front of their eyes.

If you are selling to a 'feelings' person, then you need to make them understand how they will feel when they buy your product.

For example, if you were selling them a car, you would need to communicate something like '

'Imagine how you will feel driving down the freeway with the wind in your hair, your favourite song on the radio and your family beside you. You will feel so proud of your new car.'

I will use this same car example again for each of the modalities, so we can make this concept as simple as possible.

If you want to hold a conversation with a kinaesthetic person, then again express your thoughts in a way that helps this person 'feel' their effect, because they are less likely to 'get the picture'

If you are in their environment, then at an appropriate moment ask about their family (the ones in the photos) or how they 'feel' about a relevant industry event, or a news event. Ask them about their hobbies and their life, and then extend that conversation into areas that you have learnt about them. Concentrate on how they feel about the subject.

One of the most important communication techniques, that we will learn more about later, is the art of listening. Being in the moment and really connecting with people. That will be a separate chapter, as that is a large topic to be understood in itself. Part of a great listening technique is learning to ask appropriate questions that encourage your audience to participate further in your conversation, willingly and happily sharing information, because you have made a good connection.

Remember with an audience strongly embedded in 'feeling' be sure to phrase even questions into the feeling mode.'

How do you feel about?'

'What does this mean to you?'

'Do you feel you will move towards?' etc

This type of audience will appreciate genuine warmth from you, and a feeling that you understand where they are in life. They will not appreciate fast, brash techniques, and are often more easily offended, by unfiltered, or misunderstood, words than a visual person.

If you determine the primary modality of your audience is:

Auditory

This person hears every word you say, and usually likes to talk.

When I meet a very auditory person, the first thing I notice is that they are like a waterfall. The words keep spilling, but are characteristically uncoloured, and sometimes completely disconnected to the rest of their body. Visual people will use their hands, and speak in colour with lots of adjectives to describe their picture.

Some auditory people can talk, nonstop, whilst driving, running, shopping, working, cutting up the vegetables for dinner (if I did that, I would have no fingers) and they can even talk when anyone else is talking! They do not necessarily even notice.

Sometimes, they can talk quite dispassionately, not seeming to take time to consider the feelings, they just need to describe the event in words.

Some auditory people are listeners only, they rarely speak more than a few brisk and practical words, but they hear every sound, every undertone.

Unfortunately, if you, as the speaker, are not careful they may 'hear' something you said, a slant or angle, that was not intended. It is a misinterpretation, as they may not be balancing the other modalities, of the speaker, with the words.

Most auditory people however will have strong influences from 'feelings' and/or 'visual' so they will not be so extreme. You will be able to mix a couple of modalities in your communication but try to keep auditory dominant.

The auditory audience needs you to explain, in words, very clearly exactly what your message is. This is the method that radio advertisements have to use; they are only reaching your auditory sense.

Your sentences will need to be descriptive, but without necessarily painting a traditional picture.

As you are being well heard, it is a good idea to throw in a few visual and feeling references, as they will hear them and then use their second modality to add to their understanding.

Use words like:

'I hear what you say'

'I understand what you are saying'

'This is an interesting story to listen to'

'I cannot believe I am hearing this'

'I can hear some concern in your voice'.

Your questions can be framed with examples such as:

'Can you tell me what you heard about?'

'Did you hear the item on the news about ...?'

'What did the kids/manager/neighbour tell you happened? '

'Did you hear that we launched a new product that might suit you?'

If you are selling them that car, you would need to rephrase your statement to

'Imagine driving down the freeway, listening to your favourite music with the family telling you how happy they are in the new car – by the way did you hear that motor? Sounds really safe/hot/cool (as appropriate)'

Your genuine warmth can be expressed here in a way that they can actually hear it in your words.

Use warm words, use expressive words. This is a chance to enjoy your language in an artful and interesting way, because this person will really hear you!

If you determine the primary modality of your audience is:

Visual

When your audience is dominantly visual, then you need to paint pictures with your words. This person sees their world, and what they cannot physically see, then they imagine in a picture. If you describe your new house to them, they will visualise it in their head immediately.

They will usually talk about seeing things your way, or their way.

Their language will usually be full of adjectives and descriptions that include colour, shape, style and the order of everything. This is because they speak from the picture in their minds.

If you ask them about their holiday, they will tell you what they saw. If you are not visual, then try to imagine describing a photo, and that will help you communicate with a visual person.

In their space, they are usually surrounded by visual distractions, and reminders, such as art, postcards, photos of places, holidays, events (often including family), ornamental objects, kids art, souvenirs like a bottle top from a fun party and a screen saver on their PC.

These people usually love colour, plus black and white, visual drama or 'eye candy.' Often lighting, (too much or too little), will affect their mood.

Use expressions like:

'I see'

'I want to show you'

'Let us see if we can cover that later in the presentation'

'Let me demonstrate'

You could ask questions such as:

'What do you see as your main problem?'

'What do you see as the ideal solution?'

'Where do you see this going?'

'Can you describe what you have in your mind?'

'What is your vision for...?'

To sell them that car you would have to rephrase your statement to something like;

'Imagine owning this car in gloss red with white leather, driving down the motorway and watching the mountains slide majestically by. The family looking great beside you, the GPS guiding you with ease and the look of envy from your friends when they see this red duco glistening in the sun'

Your genuine warmth needs to be seen. Your facial expression and body language are more critical than ever, as this audience is watching.

You need to have a genuine smile, and you need to show you care.

Ensure good hospitality with this kind of person if you want to impress them, because the more the surroundings match their taste, the happier and more comfortable they will be. You want them to relax and give you their attention.

Now, as I said earlier most people are a mix of modalities, so as much as you can you need to balance your communication and tailor it to suit your audience.

Let us take a look at what happens when you cannot establish a clear dominant modality, or you have a larger audience than one key person.

Now you will need to present everything, as much as possible, in all three modalities, so you do not alienate anyone. This is tricky to get right, without appearing to repeat yourself, but it is very possible.

The most outstanding public figures, that really appeal to the masses, can do this very well.

In their media interviews, they repeat their key message three times. Each time in a different abstract way, so the listeners do not notice. Why? Because each listener remembers the message in their primary modality, and mentally either does not recognise the repeats, or screens them out!

Listen to some radio or TV interviews of country presidents, or presidents of large corporations and you will see this technique demonstrated, you can learn by listening and through practice.

This does not work quite so well in a social situation, like Friday evening drinks. On these occasions you can use a modified technique.

Each time you talk about a subject, you change your modality.

You use all three methods of communicating – visual, auditory and feeling.

A sentence like 'I *heard* about the accident in the High Street, I *saw* on the news that the driver had been drinking, imagine how the store owner whose window was broken must *feel*;'

Not so difficult is it? But we rarely practice it. This will really connect you to the group you are with, on a personal level.

This technique can also work well if we are unsure of the modality of our primary audience, we can express ourselves in a way that we know he, or she, will retain the message we want to deliver.

Remember that respect for everyone we speak to, and genuine warmth towards humanity helps everyone hear, see, feel and understand our message, and our intent.

How well you can communicate at this level, will be how you are remembered, and talked about, by other people in your community, your work, and your public life. We become the messages we represent.

How well you connect, on a personal level, will determine the quality of your relationships with family, friends and impact your career. The comments of your colleagues, their respect and feeling of being connected to you, will determine your future in any industry.

Strong communication is a direct precursor to success.

In a world where everyone is talking and no one is listening, we need to use tools such as these. We need to learn to really reach out and connect with our audiences.

Then your conversations will be worthwhile, your speeches will be remembered. It will be less frustrating, and more fruitful. You will make better friends, you will be remembered as someone who listens and cares, and you will be more successful as a result.

Other Books by Terrie Anderson

The LITTLE RED SUCCESS BOOK

'Success is often judged by fame, money, possessions or position. I heartily disagree with such judgement. I believe success can only be judged by ourselves, and is based on the level of happiness we have, the peace of mind we enjoy and the goals we have set and achieved.'

An ideal companion to *30 Days of Inspiration*. This book outlines the seven secrets to success, a program that will encourage you to be a happy, successful, human being who knows how to achieve what you want out of life.

'The LITTLE RED SUCCESS BOOK is only the beginning. Its purpose is to inspire you to enter on a quest, with rewards potentially more wonderful than you have ever believed possible'

Second Edition ISBN 9780473025854 for Amazon.com

Third Edition **ISBN 978-0-9807248-2-0** Global Distribution

Available: www.terrieandersonstore.com

                        www.amazon.com

Or Order from your favourite bookstore with the global ISBN number above.

Coming Soon

Reach Out and Connect

Due for release in early 2010, this book helps you to develop effective communication skills. When you speak, people will not only listen, but they will remember the message.

It does not matter how great your message is, it is the Messenger who delivers it that will determine how the world hears it, sees it and feels about it.

90% of the impact is in the delivery.

We have more difficulty in our personal relationships if we cannot communicate effectively. If our messages are misunderstood, unheard, or forgotten then we become frustrated. Frustration, due to miscommunication, destroys many great relationships.

This is a fabulous book for anyone in sales or business, as it is a practical guide in how to reach customers and colleagues, and connect with them. It is equally useful for families with communication difficulty, or just people who do not feel their contribution is not well recognised.

Written in the usual conversational, easy to follow style of Terrie Anderson, this is a companion for anyone wanting to improve their communication.

999

Legendary Selling For the 21st Century

Are you sometimes a day late or a dollar short?

This forthright, and unquestionably direct to the point, book is for anyone who wants to absolutely excel in Sales. Forget Sales 101, 201 and 301! This is how to become a legend.

Terrie Anderson is an Australian, with an excellent reputation on three continents. She is known for her frankness, but loved for her sense of fair value, her warmth, wit and humanity. She has an enviable track record as a high achiever. She has been described in her industry as an 'Amazonian' and hired more than once by competitors because they couldn't win against her strategy and her team.

In her inimitable Aussie style, she warns this book is not for wimps, 'lazy bastards' or people who make excuses. This for people who respect sales as a profession, and really want to be the best.

This is not a typical sales book, this is about how to win, win, and win again. This is how to make serious money as a sales person, be headhunted by the competition, and best of all be loved by your customers. They will buy from you again, and again, because they respect and trust you.

Not for the feint hearted, this is a balls and all book on how to win in the big league.

Want to be a legend? Here is the how to!

Due for release in March 2010.